topps

MATCH ATTAX ®

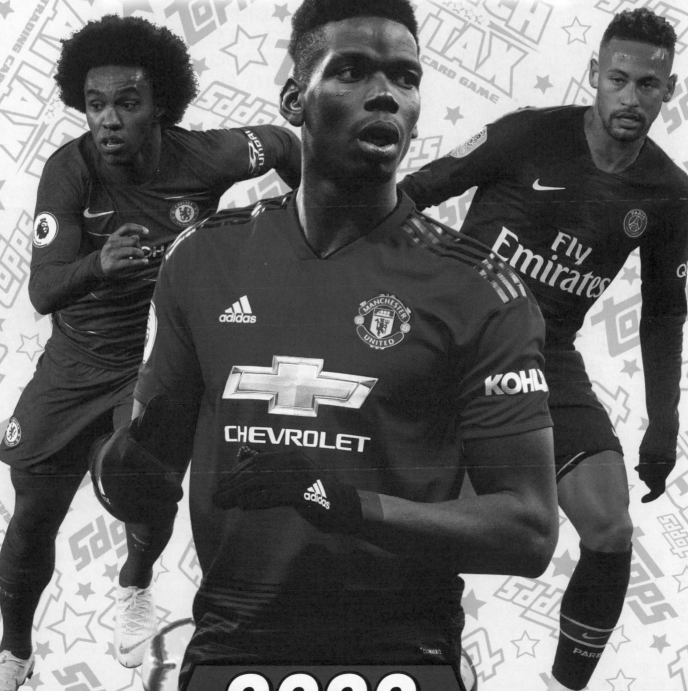

2020

With 32 wins, 98 points and 95 goals in the bag, Manchester City once again proved they were the best in the Premier League! Check out how they clinched the trophy.

MANCHESTER CITY

TEAM TALK

With probably the strongest squad in the league, boss Pep Guardiola had plenty of options to keep Manchester City in the title race. Aguero and Jesus were his main strikers, with Sterling in support, and Sane, Mahrez and Bernardo Silva operating out wide. De Bruyne struggled with injury but Gundogan got game time and teenager Foden bagged his first league goal.

SEASON STATS

POSITION: 1ST
PREMIER LEAGUE POINTS: 98
PREMIER LEAGUE WINS: 32
PREMIER LEAGUE GOALS SCORED: 95
PREMIER LEAGUE GOALS CONCEDED: 23
CLEAN SHEETS: 20
SHOTS: 683
PENALTIES SCORED: 3
PASSES: 26,581
CROSSES: 783
TACKLES: 518
YELLOW CARDS: 44
RED CARDS: 1
FOULS: 193
OFFSIDES: 98

MEGA MOMENT > > > > >

With time running out and Manchester City fearing they would drop points against Leicester City, captain Vincent Kompany became a superhero at The Etihad! The veteran defender collected the ball in front of The Foxes' goal and struck a sweet long-range effort that rifled past goalkeeper Kasper Schmeichel. Kompany's winner kept the title in reach and sent the crowd crazy!

5 EPIC STARS

SERGIO AGUERO
Aguero did his usual trick of blasting in goals, goals and goals! By May 2019 he had a mighty 164 in just 239 league games. The fans worship him!

FERNANDINHO
The midfield heartbeat, offering defensive protection and a quick brain to start attacks. He linked up superbly with the Silvas, Sane and De Bruyne.

BERNARDO SILVA
A wizard with the ball, Silva caused carnage from the wings as well as through the centre. He recorded 15 goals and assists combined – his best City stats so far!

LEROY SANE
The skilful German didn't always start, but he regularly made a big impact with his goals, assists and speed. His winner against rivals Liverpool FC was class.

EDERSON
With 20 clean sheets and having conceded just 23 goals, Ederson's second season at The Etihad confirmed his world-class talent. He's so confident in possession.

Three cheers for. uhm... me!

In 2019, **Sterling** also scored his first hat-trick for England in a 5–0 win against the Czech Republic.

PLAYER OF THE YEAR

RAHEEM STERLING

Sterling enjoyed his finest season as he clinched his second Premier League title with Manchester City. He worked his magic on the pitch, leaving defenders for dust and racing into the box to score or assist his team-mates. He was crowned PFA Young Player of the Year and the Football Writers' Association Player of the Year!

POSITION:	FORWARD
PREMIER LEAGUE GAMES:	34
PREMIER LEAGUE GOALS:	17
PASSES:	1,263
ASSISTS:	10
CROSSES:	75
RIGHT-FOOT GOALS:	11
LEFT-FOOT GOALS:	4
YELLOW CARDS:	3
RED CARDS:	0
FOULS:	40

The Reds were awesome, losing just one game all season in a tense title tussle!
Look back over their top stars, stats, goals and games.

LIVERPOOL FC

TEAM TALK

Manager Jurgen Klopp had a strong team spine to rely on, with Alisson in goal, Van Dijk in central defence and captain Henderson taking charge of midfield. The Reds' famous front three of Salah, Mane and Firmino dazzled again, grabbing 56 between them in the Premier League. New signings Fabinho and Keita impressed as the season unfolded and even squad players Shaqiri and Origi delivered moments of magic when called into the action.

SEASON STATS

POSITION: 2ND
PREMIER LEAGUE POINTS: 97
PREMIER LEAGUE WINS: 30
PREMIER LEAGUE GOALS SCORED: 89
PREMIER LEAGUE GOALS CONCEDED: 22
CLEAN SHEETS: 21
SHOTS: 575
PENALTIES SCORED: 7
PASSES: 23,638
CROSSES: 721
TACKLES: 610
YELLOW CARDS: 38
RED CARDS: 2
FOULS: 185
OFFSIDE: 77

MEGA MOMENT > > > > >

The Reds took the title fight to the last game of the season, thanks to a thriller in their second-to-last game at Newcastle United. They were drawing 2–2 with minutes left when substitute striker Divock Origi leapt high in the box to meet a cross and nodded home to snatch an unbelievable win. Sadly Liverpool FC lost the league by a single point, but moments like this will never be forgotten!

5 EPIC STARS

ANDREW ROBERTSON
Robertson became one of the best left-backs in the world! The energetic Scotsman made 11 assists, 80 tackles and 30 interceptions. Vital in defence and attack.

SADIO MANE
Mane battled with team-mate Salah to grab the Premier League Golden Boot! He finished with 22, including a crucial injury-time strike against Crystal Palace.

MOHAMED SALAH
Salah shone again, netting 22 and bagging eight assists. By the end of the season his total league record stood at an incredible 56 goals in just 87 appearances!

ALISSON
Signed in summer 2018 for around £66 million, the big Brazilian keeper showed exactly why he's worth that cash! He made superb saves all season and errors were rare.

TRENT ALEXANDER-ARNOLD
Along with Robertson, the youngster was the most eye-catching full-back in 2018–19. He made 12 assists and 201 crosses.

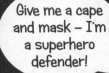
Give me a cape and mask – I'm a superhero defender!

Van Dijk was named the official Premier League **Player of the Season** for 2018–19.

PLAYER OF THE YEAR

VIRGIL VAN DIJK

Liverpool FC fans know the powerful Dutchman is the real leader in their team! In 2018–19 he played every Premier League game, keeping 20 clean sheets as they let in just 22 goals. He's a monster in the air and times tackles to perfection. Van Dijk also notched big goals for The Reds, finding the net against Newcastle United, Watford and Wolves.

POSITION:	DEFENDER
PREMIER LEAGUE GAMES:	38
PREMIER LEAGUE GOALS:	4
PASSES:	3,037
ASSISTS:	2
CLEAN SHEETS:	20
TACKLES:	38
CLEARANCES:	199
YELLOW CARDS:	1
RED CARDS:	0
FOULS:	12

The Blues scrapped for a top-four spot and, even though they weren't at their best, they still beat Manchester City, Arsenal and Tottenham Hotspur!

CHELSEA

TEAM TALK

Chelsea stuck to a 4–3–3 formation with the likes of Gonzalo Higuain, Eden Hazard and Olivier Giroud spearheading the attack at times. N'Golo Kante played in a wider midfield role and Ross Barkley, Callum Hudson-Odoi and Ruben Loftus-Cheek showed signs of their special skills going forwards. Eden Hazard and Willian were the main creative forces.

POSITION:	3RD
PREMIER LEAGUE POINTS:	72
PREMIER LEAGUE WINS:	21
PREMIER LEAGUE GOALS SCORED:	63
PREMIER LEAGUE GOALS CONCEDED:	39
CLEAN SHEETS:	16
SHOTS:	607
PENALTIES SCORED:	5
PASSES:	25,070
CROSSES:	692
TACKLES:	618
YELLOW CARDS:	49
RED CARDS:	0
FOULS:	169
OFFSIDES:	83

MEGA MOMENT > > > > >

Chelsea began 2018–19 in fantastic form, winning their first five league games and going unbeaten in 12. In early December they defeated Manchester City 2–0 at Stamford Bridge, with N'Golo Kante and David Luiz hitting the net. It was Chelsea manager Maurizio Sarri's first victory over Pep Guardiola and The Blues' fans absolutely loved causing Manchester City's first league loss of the season!

5 EPIC STARS

WILLIAN
The tricky Brazilian took his league total for goals and assists at Chelsea to more than 50. He's full of flicks, turns, dribbles and fierce long-range strikes.

PEDRO
The Spanish forward chipped in with big goals in big games throughout 2018–19, netting in important wins over London rivals Tottenham Hotspur and Arsenal.

GONZALO HIGUAIN
A goal machine around Europe, Higuain joined on loan from AC Milan and blasted a debut double against Huddersfield Town. Helped make Chelsea a threat up top.

DAVID LUIZ
Luiz won back his spot in defence after a disappointing spell in 2017–18. The Brazilian helped to keep 15 clean sheets and had a 76 per cent tackle success rate.

KEPA ARRIZABALAGA
After joining from Athletic Bilbao for a world-record £71 million, Kepa made 14 clean sheets in the league and 82 saves. He'll be stronger still in his second season!

> **Hazard** spent seven seasons at Stamford Bridge before a mega-money move to **Real Madrid** in the summer.

PLAYER OF THE YEAR

EDEN HAZARD

The brilliant Belgian was once again the star man at Stamford Bridge, clocking up more goals and assists than any of his teammates. Hazard was awesome with the ball at his feet and dribbled, flicked and dazzled his way past defenders into the box. He grabbed seven goals in six games as Chelsea enjoyed a quick-fire start to the season.

POSITION:	FORWARD
PREMIER LEAGUE GAMES:	37
PREMIER LEAGUE GOALS:	16
PASSES:	1,819
ASSISTS:	15
CROSSES:	145
RIGHT-FOOT GOALS:	11
LEFT-FOOT GOALS:	5
YELLOW CARDS:	2
RED CARDS:	0
FOULS:	12

BOOT THE NET!

Arsenal ace **Alexandre Lacazette** collected 27 goals and 12 assists in his first 67 league games for The Gunners!

```
                                    C   N   L
                                        Z
                            R   T   D   H   O
                                H       D   V
                            E   Y   X   B   Y
                                Z   B   C   D
                    L           Y   C   N   E
W   S   Z   A   C   E   W   X   L   E   I   T   D   Z
J   B   T   D   F   I   Z   N   E   M   R   H   D   Z
F   E   O   E   L   A   A   V   M   V   E   E   H   O
B   R   S   S   R   M   Y   E   N   A   T   E   D   V
C   W   O   U   G   L   J   S   E   L   T   X   B   Y
J   N   W   J   S   O   I   A   N   A   Z   B   C   D
K   U   Q   H   V   E   U   N   A   F   G   Q   R   R
U   X   T   I   I   G   T   D   L   G   X   A   X   A
V   U   L   H   M   C   J   E   W   E   Y   C   P   V
V   I   C   F   P   A   W   R   Y   T   E   W   I   C
M   C   I   O   N   H   X   S   T   S   W   I   G
Y   H   D   C   D   B   Y   O   G   A   S   P   D   V
A   D   Y   B   S   O   L   N   W   S   R   D   S
R   I   C   H   A   R   L   I   S   O   N   L   P
H   A   S   P   E   W   Y   U   W   E   F   T   Z
```

Spot these red-hot Premier League goal-grabbers stuffed inside the boot!

MANE
STERLING
SON
WILSON
ANDERSON
JESUS
DEENEY
VARDY
MILIVOJEVIC

RICHARLISON
MURRAY
WILLIAN
LACAZETTE
FIRMINO
MARTIAL
MOURA
JIMENEZ

Yep, I'm the Mane man at Anfield!

Liverpool FC star **Sadio Mane** finished the 2018–19 season as the Premier League's joint top scorer with 22 goals.

```
W  S  Z
S  B     T     D
F  U  U  T  O  D  E        L
F  Y  A  L  R  D  E  R     U     M
E  V  V  L  R  Q  R     L  F     M  M  V     N     X     O
P  T  T  R  R  R  R     L  O     H  J     A     N     L     C     M
A  G  G  T  T  R  U     D  O     O  O     I     M     T     B     U     J
I  R  R  R  R  R  E     I  U     V  M     L     M     E     T     X     I
A  A  A  H  H  F  M     R  Z     R  J     L     U     E     U     R     S
N  X  X  X  F     I     A  R     I     L     M     E     I     N     B     F
F  P  P  Y  F     H  M  C     W     O     W     M     B     E     I
X  M  M  V  W     B  D  U     A     O     I     O     I     I     Z
M  A  A  R  T     I  A  L     S     L     T     A     Z     V
N  M  M  E  O     N  B  A     U     Z     Q     A     X     L
X  J  J  L  F     P  H  V     V     W     R     N     Q     Z
```

ANSWERS ON PAGE 55.

Spurs' sick style and talented players guided them to another top-four finish. Take a look over their biggest matches and the super stats and facts of 2018–19.

TOTTENHAM HOTSPUR

TEAM TALK

With Alderweireld and Vertonghen one of the best defensive duos in the league, boss Mauricio Pochettino could use Winks and Sissoko as midfield protection. That allowed creative heroes like Eriksen, Moura, Dele Alli and Lamela to set up chances for Kane and Son. Trippier was a handy attacking outlet from full-back down the right wing.

SEASON STATS

POSITION:	4TH
PREMIER LEAGUE POINTS:	71
PREMIER LEAGUE WINS:	23
PREMIER LEAGUE GOALS SCORED:	67
PREMIER LEAGUE GOALS CONCEDED:	39
CLEAN SHEETS:	13
SHOTS:	537
PENALTIES SCORED:	4
PASSES:	21,295
CROSSES:	643
TACKLES:	626
YELLOW CARDS:	56
RED CARDS:	3
FOULS:	225
OFFSIDES:	74

MEGA MOMENT >>>>>

Tottenham Hotspur smashed Everton for six away from home, but their best away display was a 3–0 win at Manchester United. The Londoners outclassed The Red Devils and two quick goals from Kane and Moura at the start of the second half set them up. Moura's second strike late on gave Spurs their third win in a row as they made an early-season title charge.

5 EPIC STARS

HEUNG-MIN SON
Son has reached double figures for goals in the last three seasons for Spurs. The fearsome South Korea forward also struck six assists in 2018–19!

CHRISTIAN ERIKSEN
Spurs are much more dangerous when Eriksen is in the side. The Dane's dribbling, speed, set pieces and long-range shooting are totally top class!

TOBY ALDERWEIRELD
The powerful defender kept 12 clean sheets as the focus of Spurs' defence. In 2018–19 he only missed four matches and had a 65 per cent tackle success.

LUCAS MOURA
In his first full season for Tottenham Hotspur, the Brazil midfielder displayed his sweet skills and ability to race into the box. Played wide and central.

DELE ALLI
The England ace was hit by injuries, but he still tapped in five goals and was a vital link player for the strikers. Scored in big wins over Chelsea and Everton.

Watch out – there's a Hurri-Kane blowing in!

Kane scooped the famous FIFA World Cup Golden Boot trophy as the top scorer in 2018 with **six goals** for England.

PLAYER OF THE YEAR

HARRY KANE

Kane's attacking stats are as good as ever! In his 28 league games last season, he netted 17 goals before injury ended his season. He made four assists and had 46 shots on target. In 2018–19 the England captain never went more than three Premier League games without scoring and netted against Manchester United, Arsenal and Chelsea.

POSITION:	FORWARD
PREMIER LEAGUE GAMES:	28
PREMIER LEAGUE GOALS:	17
PASSES:	551
ASSISTS:	4
CROSSES:	12
RIGHT-FOOT GOALS:	12
LEFT-FOOT GOALS:	3
YELLOW CARDS:	5
RED CARDS:	0
FOULS:	31

Under new manager Unai Emery, The Gunners enjoyed some great wins with exciting players showing off their skills. Check out their facts and stats.

Erm, are we shooting this way?

ARSENAL

TEAM TALK

Arsenal lost their first two league fixtures, but then went on a run of 14 games without defeat. Kolasinac and Monreal battled for the left-back role with Sokratis, Mustafi or Koscielny taking up the two centre-back spots in a flat back four. Lacazette and Aubameyang often started together with Mkhitaryan, Iwobi and Ramsey threading forward passes.

SEASON STATS

POSITION:	5TH
PREMIER LEAGUE POINTS:	70
PREMIER LEAGUE WINS:	21
PREMIER LEAGUE GOALS SCORED:	73
PREMIER LEAGUE GOALS CONCEDED:	51
CLEAN SHEETS:	8
SHOTS:	467
PENALTIES SCORED:	4
PASSES:	20,805
CROSSES:	605
TACKLES:	609
YELLOW CARDS:	72
RED CARDS:	2
FOULS:	227
OFFSIDES:	89

MEGA MOMENT

During Arsenal's 14-game unbeaten league run, they smashed north-London rivals Spurs 4–2 at The Emirates. An Aubameyang double, plus finishes from Lacazette and Torreira, secured the three points. Arsenal also enjoyed a sweet 2–0 win over Chelsea in January, but beating Tottenham Hotspur is always top of a Gunners fan's wishlist!

5 EPIC STARS

ALEXANDRE LACAZETTE
The Frenchman was often used as part of a two-man attack, with Aubameyang playing just behind. His coolness in the box was impressive.

HENRIKH MKHITARYAN
Mkhitaryan outshone Ozil to clock up ten goals and assists in total. His sharp brain and precise passing gave the forwards ammunition.

MATTEO GUENDOUZI
Guendouzi proved to be a £7 million bargain, playing 33 games and tackling and pressing hard in front of his defence. Needs to add goals to his game now.

SOKRATIS
He became The Gunners' top centre-back, clocking five clean sheets with 108 clearances and 26 interceptions. He was missed when he was injured in late January.

HECTOR BELLERIN
Arsenal's first-choice right-back reached 143 league appearances and chipped in with five assists and 785 passes. Bursting with speed and well-timed tackles!

Aubameyang and **Mkhitaryan** are a sharp mix for Arsenal. They first starred together playing for **Borussia Dortmund** in Germany!

PLAYER OF THE YEAR

PIERRE-EMERICK AUBAMEYANG

The super striker jointly won the Golden Boot in 2018–19 with 22 goals. In his first 49 league games for Arsenal, he bagged 32 goals and nine assists. Aubameyang was Player of the Month in October and his skillled strikes with his right, left and from the penalty spot makes him a deadly finisher. Linking up with Lacazette and Mkhitaryan gives Arsenal the firepower to make defenders weep!

POSITION:	FORWARD
PREMIER LEAGUE GAMES:	36
PREMIER LEAGUE GOALS:	22
PASSES:	692
ASSISTS:	5
CROSSES:	43
RIGHT-FOOT GOALS:	20
LEFT-FOOT GOALS:	2
YELLOW CARDS:	0
RED CARDS:	0
FOULS:	13

With Pogba, Lingard, Rashford and Lukaku, The Red Devils have a quality attacking team that can take on the best! Find out the story of their season.

MANCHESTER UNITED

TEAM TALK

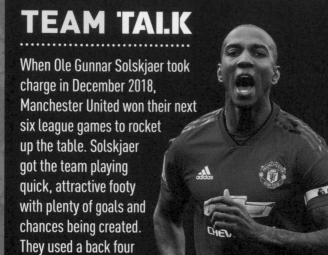

When Ole Gunnar Solskjaer took charge in December 2018, Manchester United won their next six league games to rocket up the table. Solskjaer got the team playing quick, attractive footy with plenty of goals and chances being created. They used a back four and three forwards, with Pogba bossing the midfield and the full-backs pressing down the wings.

SEASON STATS

POSITION: 6TH
PREMIER LEAGUE POINTS: 66
PREMIER LEAGUE WINS: 19
PREMIER LEAGUE GOALS SCORED: 65
PREMIER LEAGUE GOALS CONCEDED: 54
CLEAN SHEETS: 7
SHOTS: 526
PENALTIES SCORED: 9
PASSES: 19,202
CROSSES: 638
TACKLES: 581
YELLOW CARDS: 73
RED CARDS: 4
FOULS: 221
OFFSIDES: 90

MEGA MOMENT > > > > >

Solskjaer scored 126 goals as a Manchester United player. As soon as he took over from Jose Mourinho, The Red Devils looked like a different team that wanted to get into the box and cause damage. Ole won his first game 5-1 at Cardiff and he didn't lose a Premier League match until a 2-0 defeat to Arsenal in March. Their season faded, but he certainly saved it!

5 EPIC STARS

ANTHONY MARTIAL
The flying France forward hit top gear in October through to December, scoring eight in just ten games. He finished with ten strikes and two assists.

MARCUS RASHFORD
The former youth star edged ahead of Romelu Lukaku in the striking pecking order. Rashford was amazing down the wings, dribbling into the box or leading the line.

LUKE SHAW
Shaw bounced back to show the form that makes him one of the best all-round defenders in the league. Made four assists and 52 crosses into the box.

DAVID DE GEA
The Spain star made 122 saves and played every Premier League game. He took some criticism, but de Gea's been a big influence at Old Trafford since 2011!

JESSE LINGARD
With his speed, passing, dribbling, long-range shooting and clever assists, Lingard's a hero at Old Trafford. His goal celebrations are pretty special, too!

Pogba went goal crazy when Solskjaer took charge, grabbing four goals in the manager's first three games!

PLAYER OF THE YEAR

PAUL POGBA

The FIFA World Cup winner had a big season at Old Trafford, being directly involved in 22 league goals. He bagged doubles against Huddersfield Town, AFC Bournemouth and Fulham and completed over 2,000 passes and made 28 crosses. He had a quiet end to the season, but when he's in top gear Pogba is one of the best all-action midfielders in world footy!

POSITION:	MIDFIELDER
PREMIER LEAGUE GAMES:	35
PREMIER LEAGUE GOALS:	13
PASSES:	2,068
ASSISTS:	9
CROSSES:	28
RIGHT-FOOT GOALS:	11
LEFT-FOOT GOALS	1
YELLOW CARDS:	6
RED CARDS:	0
FOULS:	54

Wolves stormed back into the Premier League and became one of the most thrilling teams to watch! With their super signings and sick style, this team is aiming high.

WOLVERHAMPTON WANDERERS

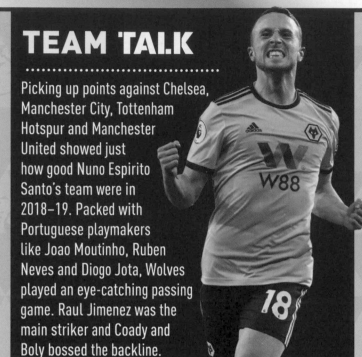

TEAM TALK

Picking up points against Chelsea, Manchester City, Tottenham Hotspur and Manchester United showed just how good Nuno Espirito Santo's team were in 2018–19. Packed with Portuguese playmakers like Joao Moutinho, Ruben Neves and Diogo Jota, Wolves played an eye-catching passing game. Raul Jimenez was the main striker and Coady and Boly bossed the backline.

SEASON STATS

- **POSITION:** 7TH
- **PREMIER LEAGUE POINTS:** 57
- **PREMIER LEAGUE WINS:** 16
- **PREMIER LEAGUE GOALS SCORED:** 47
- **PREMIER LEAGUE GOALS CONCEDED:** 46
- **CLEAN SHEETS:** 9
- **SHOTS:** 477
- **PENALTIES SCORED:** 4
- **PASSES:** 16,618
- **CROSSES:** 622
- **TACKLES:** 720
- **YELLOW CARDS:** 72
- **RED CARDS:** 1
- **FOULS:** 223
- **OFFSIDES:** 73

MEGA MOMENT >>>>>

Nuno Espirito Santo steered Wolverhampton Wanderers to a memorable 3–1 win against Tottenham Hotspur at Wembley. Wolves were behind with 18 minutes to go before goals from Boly, Jimenez and Costa sealed the shock win. It made the rest of the league really respect the newcomers as a genuine top-ten team, while Jimenez's finish capped a cool team move.

5 EPIC STARS

WILLY BOLY
Goals against Newcastle United, Tottenham Hotspur and Manchester City earned Wolves vital points. Boly was immense in defence and well worth his transfer fee.

JONNY
Wolves snapped up the left-sided star in January 2019 after he joined on loan in the summer from Atletico Madrid. Jonny has quality tackling and passing in his locker!

MATT DOHERTY
One of the best wing-backs of the season, Doherty was involved in nine league goals for Wolves. Speedy, accurate and always a threat from set pieces.

JOAO MOUTINHO
With over 100 Portugal caps, Moutinho has the experience and skills to boss Wolves' midfield. He struck eight assists and netted a big goal at Old Trafford in the league.

DIOGO JOTA
The elegant attacker was at it again in 2018–19, scoring classy strikes against Chelsea and Newcastle United and an epic hat-trick to beat Leicester City!

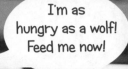

I'm as hungry as a wolf! Feed me now!

Raul Jimenez was so impressive that in April, Wolves agreed to pay Benfica a club record **£30 million** to sign him permanently!

PLAYER OF THE YEAR

RAUL JIMENEZ

Master Mexico marksman Jimenez scored headers, penalties, tap-ins and power-packed drills for Wolves in 2018–19 while originally on loan from Benfica. The club's top scorer was a nightmare for defenders, and his all-round game impressed fans as he clocked up seven assists and linked up superbly with the midfielders and forwards.

POSITION:	FORWARD
PREMIER LEAGUE GAMES:	38
PREMIER LEAGUE GOALS:	13
PASSES:	1,059
ASSISTS:	7
CROSSES:	27
RIGHT-FOOT GOALS:	9
LEFT-FOOT GOALS:	1
YELLOW CARDS:	4
RED CARDS:	0
FOULS:	42

The Toffees dream of being a top-six team and in 2018–19 they showed signs of the type of footy that could finally bring glory back to Goodison Park!

EVERTON

Not fair! Mum says it's my bedtime!

TEAM TALK

Playing with a lone striker, three supporting forwards, defensive midfielders and a back four, Everton worked hard to deliver exciting and attacking footy for the fans. Idrissa Gueye conducted central midfield, Kurt Zouma and Michael Keane created a strong central defence and left-back Lucas Digne became a big star with his fab free-kicks. Jordan Pickford kept his No.1 spot.

SEASON STATS

POSITION:	8TH
PREMIER LEAGUE POINTS:	54
PREMIER LEAGUE WINS:	15
PREMIER LEAGUE GOALS SCORED:	54
PREMIER LEAGUE GOALS CONCEDED:	46
CLEAN SHEETS:	14
SHOTS:	498
PENALTIES SCORED:	2
PASSES:	16,494
CROSSES:	814
TACKLES:	700
YELLOW CARDS:	55
RED CARDS:	4
FOULS:	250
OFFSIDES:	69

MEGA MOMENT >>>>>>

Everton recorded their biggest win of the season with a 5–1 bashing of Burnley on Boxing Day. Mina, Digne (2), Sigurdsson and Richarlison were on the score sheet as The Toffees dominated the game at Turf Moor. It was the perfect Christmas present for Everton following a heavy defeat by Tottenham Hotspur.

5 EPIC STARS

IDRISSA GUEYE
Gueye was so red-hot that Ligue 1 giants PSG tried to buy him in January! He averaged over 50 passes per game and made more than 140 tackles in total.

GYLFI SIGURDSSON
The cool Iceland hero was full of goals, assists and clever passing in 2018–19. Sigurdsson linked up well with Richarlison in front of him.

MICHAEL KEANE
The England defender clocked up his 100th Premier League game and was manager Marco Silva's No.1 centre-back. Tough in the air, he guarded his area well.

ANDRE GOMES
Signed on loan from Barcelona, Portugal midfielder Gomes became a major attacking threat for Everton. Gomes can ping passes and intercept play with tidy tackles.

LUCAS DIGNE
What a lethal left foot this French defender has! He rescued a point against Watford with a wonderful free-kick and also found the back of the net twice at Burnley.

Richarlison bagged his first strikes for Brazil, too, last season in a 5–0 thumping of El Salvador!

PLAYER OF THE YEAR

RICHARLISON

Richarlison joined Everton in an eye-popping move from Watford that cost around £50 million! The dangerous forward hit the net early on, against Wolverhampton Wanderers and Southampton, and also winners over Leicester City and Brighton & Hove Albion. With pace, power and cool finishing, Richarlison can worry any defence for 90 minutes!

POSITION:	FORWARD
PREMIER LEAGUE GAMES:	35
PREMIER LEAGUE GOALS:	13
PASSES:	793
ASSISTS:	1
CROSSES:	47
RIGHT-FOOT GOALS:	7
LEFT-FOOT GOALS:	4
YELLOW CARDS:	5
RED CARDS:	1
FOULS:	32

HIT OR MISS?

Did these super strikes in the 2018–19 season actually cross the goal line... or not?

1

Eden Hazard fires for Chelsea from a tight angle against Huddersfield Town.

- IT WAS A GOAL.
- IT WASN'T A GOAL.

AFC Bournemouth midfielder, Andrew Surman, shoots from distance against Cardiff City.

- IT WAS A GOAL.
- IT WASN'T A GOAL.

2

③

Celtic's Jozo Simunovic tries to knock the ball past the St Johnstone keeper.

IT WAS A GOAL.

IT WASN'T A GOAL.

Did Leicester City's Jamie Vardy beat the Burnley defence here?

IT WAS A GOAL.

IT WASN'T A GOAL.

④

⑤

Everton captain Seamus Coleman drills an effort against Brighton & Hove Albion.

IT WAS A GOAL.

IT WASN'T A GOAL.

ANSWERS ON PAGE 55.

The Foxes enjoyed a fifth Premier League season in a row and finished safely in mid-table, helped by awesome wins over Manchester City and Chelsea!

LEICESTER CITY

TEAM TALK

Brendan Rodgers' 4-1-4-1 system, with lone striker Jamie Vardy supported by the likes of James Maddison, Demarai Gray and Harvey Barnes, had great success. Club captain Wes Morgan, Harry Maguire and Jonny Evans competed for the centre-back spots as Wilfred Ndidi and Nampalys Mendy offered midfield protection. The Foxes' full-backs pushed forwards as they tried to win games using Vardy's counter-attacking pace.

SEASON STATS

POSITION:	9TH
PREMIER LEAGUE POINTS:	52
PREMIER LEAGUE WINS:	15
PREMIER LEAGUE GOALS SCORED:	51
PREMIER LEAGUE GOALS CONCEDED:	48
CLEAN SHEETS:	10
SHOTS:	515
PENALTIES SCORED:	5
PASSES:	17,219
CROSSES:	779
TACKLES:	676
YELLOW CARDS:	57
RED CARDS:	5
FOULS:	210
OFFSIDES:	72

MEGA MOMENT > > > > >

Fresh from a 1–0 win at Stamford Bridge just before Christmas, Leicester City enjoyed another gift of three points at Manchester City on Boxing Day! Despite falling behind, The Foxes fought back for a 2–1 victory, with goals from Marc Albrighton and the impressive Ricardo Pereira. It helped them forget the 5–1 thrashing at The Etihad earlier in 2018!

5 EPIC STARS

RICARDO PEREIRA
The Portugal star is a versatile and exciting full-back who can also play on the wings, using his speed and sharp control to link up with the attackers.

JAMES MADDISON
Costing over £22 million, the skilful forward repaid The Foxes with goals, assists and match-winning displays. Named in the England squad for the first time.

BEN CHILWELL
In 2018–19 the left-back made his England debut and only missed two Premier League games. Chilwell put in over 130 crosses as he attacked down the wing.

HARRY MAGUIRE
As powerful and commanding as ever. Maguire made 31 tackles, five blocks and popped up with three goals, including a late winner at Southampton.

WILFRED NDIDI
It's no surprise that Leicester City gave the Nigerian a huge new six-year deal – he's one of the best defensive midfielders in the Premier League!

In his career, **Jamie Vardy** has won the official Premier League Player of the Season, Goal of the Month and Player of the Month awards!

PLAYER OF THE YEAR

JAMIE VARDY

The Foxes' leading striker once again, scoring 18 goals and making four assists in 2018–19. Vardy took his overall tally to 80 in 176 Premier League games. The former England star began to thrive under Rodgers, bagging six in six games when the boss first took charge in late February. Vardy is still the goal king at the King Power Stadium!

POSITION:	FORWARD
PREMIER LEAGUE GAMES:	34
PREMIER LEAGUE GOALS:	18
PASSES:	416
ASSISTS:	4
CROSSES:	28
RIGHT-FOOT GOALS:	11
LEFT-FOOT GOALS:	4
YELLOW CARDS:	3
RED CARDS:	1
FOULS:	19

The Hammers had an up and down season, but wins over Manchester United and Arsenal showed they can mix it with the Premier League big guns!

WEST HAM UNITED

TEAM TALK

Experienced manager Manuel Pellegrini made tweaks to his formation. He often used Marko Arnautovic as a lone striker, but sometimes Javier Hernandez came in as a supporting forward. Declan Rice and Mark Noble patrolled central midfield, with Felipe Anderson, Robert Snodgrass and Michail Antonio breaking into the box. West Ham United scored more goal than Leicester City, Newcastle United and Burnley.

SEASON STATS

POSITION: 10TH
PREMIER LEAGUE POINTS: 52
PREMIER LEAGUE WINS: 15
PREMIER LEAGUE GOALS SCORED: 52
PREMIER LEAGUE GOALS CONCEDED: 55
CLEAN SHEETS: 7
SHOTS: 441
PENALTIES SCORED: 5
PASSES: 16,358
CROSSES: 630
TACKLES: 723
YELLOW CARDS: 59
RED CARDS: 1
FOULS: 182
OFFSIDES: 72

MEGA MOMENT >>>>>

West Ham United's 2-0 win at Fulham in December was their fourth in a row in the league. It was nearly five years since the club last matched that run! The Hammers cracked in 11 goals in those games as they began to look at a top-ten finish. Another ace match was their goal-crazy 8-0 League Cup victory over Macclesfield Town!

5 EPIC STARS

DECLAN RICE
The combative midfielder or defender only turned 20 in 2019 and has a big future at the London Stadium. He's brave, clever with the ball and full of energy.

MICHAIL ANTONIO
The versatile midfielder took a while to find his scoring boots. When he did, he struck against Cardiff, Fulham and Liverpool FC to collect precious points.

MARKO ARNAUTOVIC
The big Austrian showed off his strength, skills and finishing. He was involved in 14 league goals and rescued a draw at home to Brighton & Hove Albion.

LUKASZ FABIANSKI
Signed from Swansea City for just £7 million, the former Arsenal stopper was calm between the sticks. Lukasz made 148 saves and kept seven clean sheets.

ISSA DIOP
The £22 million young French defender built an impressive reputation in the heart of defence and helped keep The Hammers well away from relegation.

Filipe Anderson really is the golden boy at West Ham United – he won an Olympic gold medal with Brazil in 2016!

First prize in the Silly Face competition, too!

PLAYER OF THE YEAR

FELIPE ANDERSON

West Ham United splashed £36 million on Anderson. He took time to get going at the London Stadium, but his cheeky flicked goal against Manchester United showed his talent. The attacker bagged nine goals, four assists and recorded 25 shots on target. Whether finishing with his right or left, Anderson caused carnage for keepers!

POSITION:	MIDFIELDER
PREMIER LEAGUE GAMES:	36
PREMIER LEAGUE GOALS:	9
PASSES:	1,667
ASSISTS:	4
CROSSES:	121
RIGHT-FOOT GOALS:	6
LEFT-FOOT GOALS:	3
YELLOW CARDS:	3
RED CARDS:	0
FOULS:	27

The Hornets hovered comfortably in mid-table and once again flexed their Premier League muscle with big wins against big teams!

WATFORD

We had a glove-ly season!

TEAM TALK

After Richarlison left for Everton, Watford shared goals around the team with Deeney, Deulofeu and Pereyra scoring 25 between them. Boss Javi Gracia often kept his team narrow and compact to frustrate the opposition, with a 4-2-2-2 formation much of the time. Deeney chased long balls and skilful midfielders ghosted into the penalty area in support.

SEASON STATS

POSITION: 11TH
PREMIER LEAGUE POINTS: 50
PREMIER LEAGUE WINS: 14
PREMIER LEAGUE GOALS SCORED: 52
PREMIER LEAGUE GOALS CONCEDED: 59
CLEAN SHEETS: 7
SHOTS: 437
PENALTIES SCORED: 1
PASSES: 15,462
CROSSES: 570
TACKLES: 655
YELLOW CARDS: 77
RED CARDS: 4
FOULS: 231
OFFSIDES: 89

MEGA MOMENT > > > > >

Watford fans were in dreamland at the start of 2018-19! A 2-1 win against Tottenham Hotspur was the club's fourth in a row and they sat joint top of the table, ahead of teams like Arsenal and Manchester United. A return to European football looked possible and Watford's style and work-rate were applauded by fans around the league.

5 EPIC STARS

ETIENNE CAPOUE
The Frenchman protected his defence superbly with tackles, clearances and aerial battles. Formed an awesome midfield pairing with Doucoure.

TROY DEENEY
As well as being involved in 14 league goals, plus an FA Cup semi-final winner, the Watford captain worked tirelessly for the team in every game.

BEN FOSTER
Although he turned 36 in 2018-19, Foster reached 300 Premier League games, proving he's still a class act. He made 127 saves and kept seven clean sheets.

ABDOULAYE DOUCOURE
The all-action midfielder was a vital part of Watford's success. The popular Frenchman struck five times and loved to power headed goals into the net!

ROBERTO PEREYRA
The Argentine had his most effective season at Vicarage Road, scoring in wins over Brighton & Hove Albion, Crystal Palace, Wolves and Huddersfield Town.

Deulofeu's hat-trick in February 2019 was Watford's first in the top flight since 1986!

PLAYER OF THE YEAR

GERARD DEULOFEU

The Spaniard's first Premier League hat-trick in a 5–1 win at Cardiff caught the eye, but his displays were top class all season. Deulofeu played in a range of roles and was happy to drift wide, win the ball, cross into the box or drive past defenders. Fans will never forget his heroic goals in the FA Cup semi-final against Wolves!

POSITION:	MIDFIELDER
PREMIER LEAGUE GAMES:	30
PREMIER LEAGUE GOALS:	10
PASSES:	718
ASSISTS:	5
CROSSES:	62
RIGHT-FOOT GOALS:	10
LEFT-FOOT GOALS:	0
YELLOW CARDS:	3
RED CARDS:	0
FOULS:	14

The Eagles flew nicely above the relegation zone and finished in 12th place. Take a look at their big stars, top results and team tactics.

CRYSTAL PALACE

TEAM TALK

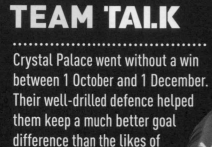

Crystal Palace went without a win between 1 October and 1 December. Their well-drilled defence helped them keep a much better goal difference than the likes of AFC Bournemouth, Burnley and Southampton around them in the table. Scott Dann's return after injury in 2019 helped keep them tough at the back and loan signing Michy Batshuayi added fresh firepower and pace.

SEASON STATS

POSITION:	12TH
PREMIER LEAGUE POINTS:	49
PREMIER LEAGUE WINS:	14
PREMIER LEAGUE GOALS SCORED:	51
PREMIER LEAGUE GOALS CONCEDED:	53
CLEAN SHEETS:	12
SHOTS:	493
PENALTIES SCORED:	10
PASSES:	15,243
CROSSES:	577
TACKLES:	730
YELLOW CARDS:	58
RED CARDS:	2
FOULS:	224
OFFSIDE:	78

MEGA MOMENT >>>>>

Schlupp, Townsend and Milivojevic struck as The Eagles flew away with an amazing 3–2 win at Manchester City. The shock result gave Crystal Palace their first back-to-back victories of the season. They also enjoyed a 3–1 win away at Burnley in March as they moved clear of the relegation spots.

5 EPIC STARS

AARON WAN-BISSAKA
The right-back rocked it for The Eagles all season! He was tough in tackles, tidy with his passing and broke forward whenever he got the chance.

LUKA MILIVOJEVIC
Crystal Palace's mega captain was on top of his game in 2018–19. Setting up attacks and whipping in crosses, he notched 12 goals and is a penalty ace.

JAMES McARTHUR
One of the unsung heroes in Crystal Palace's midfield. The hard-working Scot struck three goals in the league and an impressive six assists.

ANDROS TOWNSEND
The eye-catching midfielder showed the form that made him an England star a few years ago. He scored against Chelsea, Manchester City and Liverpool FC.

JAMES TOMKINS
Playing with Mamadou Sakho in central defence, Tomkins only missed nine league games and helped The Eagles keep nine clean sheets last season.

In over 170 Premier League appearances, **Zaha** has only ever scored one headed goal!

PLAYER OF THE YEAR

WILFRIED ZAHA

The fancy footwork, dribbling and ace shooting of the Crystal Palace forward made him the man to watch at Selhurst Park. Zaha played wide and supported the strikers, and his goals in 2019 against Southampton, West Ham United, Leicester City and Burnley were vital for The Eagles.

POSITION:	FORWARD
PREMIER LEAGUE GAMES:	34
PREMIER LEAGUE GOALS:	10
PASSES:	1,006
ASSISTS:	5
CROSSES:	37
RIGHT-FOOT GOALS:	8
LEFT-FOOT GOALS:	2
YELLOW CARDS:	8
RED CARDS:	1
FOULS:	44

EPIC EUROPEAN ACTION!

Count my league titles – all ten of 'em!

Check out the top teams and stars from Spain, Germany, France and Italy in 2018–19!

LA LIGA

No one could stop the mighty Barcelona sweeping up their 26th La Liga title and seventh this decade. Messi and Luis Suarez mesmerized up front, scoring 57 between them in the league as Barca lost just three games all season. Ousmane Dembele and Philippe Coutinho began to repay their mighty price tags in attack and Gerard Pique patrolled the backline with his cool skills and power.

BUNDESLIGA

Surprise defeats saw Bayern Munich drop to fifth in the table early on, but the serial champions bounced back, and a 5–0 win over Borussia Dortmund in April put them in pole position. Striker Robert Lewandowski blasted 22 goals, with Serge Gnabry, Thomas Muller, Leon Goretzka and James Rodriguez chipping in too. Jadon Sancho's Borussia Dortmund finished as runners-up with RB Leipzig third.

Cristiano Ronaldo became the first player to win the league title in Italy, Spain and England.

LIGUE 1

SERIE A

With £200 million superstar Neymar injured between January and April, World Cup winner Mbappe carried on his red-hot scoring form for champions Paris Saint-Germain. He scored hat-tricks over Monaco and Guingamp, plus a four-goal strike against Lyon. Neymar and Edinson Cavani grabbed over 30 league goals between them and winger Angel Di Maria reached double figures for assists. Lille, Lyon and Saint-Etienne trailed behind the French giants.

With just four defeats and finishing 11 points ahead of second-placed Napoli, Juventus cruised to the Italian crown in 2019. Cristiano Ronaldo cost £99 million, but he repaid that with 21 goals and eight assists. Joao Cancelo, Mario Mandzukic, Alex Sandro, Paulo Dybala and Miralem Pjanic were regular star players in Turin. Atalanta and Inter Milan grabbed the other two Champions League spots.

CAPTAIN

Time to name these Premier League players who all wore the captain's armband in 2018–19. Take a look at the clues if you need a little help!

TEASERS!

I didn't 'skip' any questions!

1

ANSWER ....

2

ANSWER ....

3

ANSWER ....

4

ANSWER ....

5

ANSWER ....

6

ANSWER ....

7

ANSWER ....

8

ANSWER ....

1. A devilish defender, I'm young at heart.
2. This French skipper's Gunner get you!
3. This legend doesn't need a Pep talk!
4. Myths Timmo is an anagram of my name!
5. My first name is James!
6. The start of my surname is as easy as A to Z!
7. This great Scot's home is a Cottage!
8. It's cold – put the 'heat on'!
9. I Spur my team on to keep a clean sheet!
10. My fave birds are Magpies!
11. Fancy a game of Simon Says?
12. This skipper shares his name with a supermarket!
13. My name rhymes with Les Borgan!
14. Mark my words – I'll Hammer the ball home!
15. You can call me Double C!
16. My name is a famous jumping move in basketball!

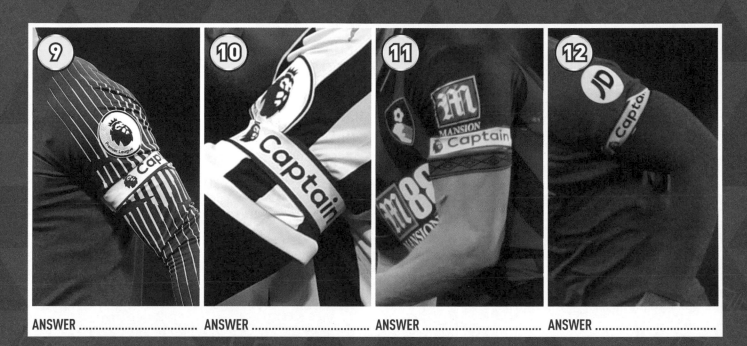

ANSWER .... ANSWER .... ANSWER .... ANSWER ....

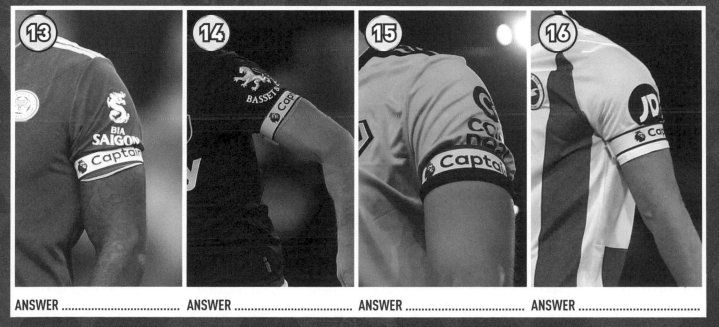

ANSWER .... ANSWER .... ANSWER .... ANSWER ....

ANSWERS ON PAGE 55.

The Magpies once again did enough to keep Premier League footy at St. James' Park. Discover the goal stars, creative midfielders and tough defenders who did the business!

NEWCASTLE UNITED

TEAM TALK

Newcastle United had a terrible start, not winning any of their first ten league games, but bounced back to become a tough team to crack. Boss Rafa Benitez used both a five- and four-man defence, with Rondon and Perez in attack. Box-to-box midfielder Ki Sung-Yueng had annoying injuries but Senegal star Mohamed Diame was consistent in his defensive midfield role.

SEASON STATS

POSITION:	13TH
PREMIER LEAGUE POINTS:	45
PREMIER LEAGUE WINS:	12
PREMIER LEAGUE GOALS SCORED:	42
PREMIER LEAGUE GOALS CONCEDED:	48
CLEAN SHEETS:	11
SHOTS:	446
PENALTIES SCORED:	1
PASSES:	13,490
CROSSES:	711
TACKLES:	714
YELLOW CARDS:	57
RED CARDS:	2
FOULS:	266
OFFSIDE:	59

MEGA MOMENT > > > > > >

The Magpies' win over Manchester City in January was epic, but beating Burnley in November was even more important. It was the club's third win in a row and lifted them to 13th in the table. Ben Mee's own goal and a Ciaran Clark header did the damage in the first half as Newcastle United picked up their first away win of the season.

5 EPIC STARS

JAMAAL LASCELLES
The captain was Newcastle United's rock. Lascelles helped to keep 11 clean sheets, had a 66 per cent tackle success and made 213 clearances.

MATT RITCHIE
Whether playing wing-back or midfield, Ritchie remained one of Newcastle United's creative stars. The Scot made eight assists and scored two goals.

SEAN LONGSTAFF
The midfielder only made his Premier League debut on Boxing Day, but went on to play nine games and scored against Burnley. Calm and composed.

AYOZE PEREZ
Perez was lively in attack all season, having 55 shots and scoring 12 goals. He netted winners against Watford and Leicester City, plus a hat-trick v The Saints!

FABIAN SCHAR
The defender took a while to settle, but his passing, power and knack of scoring means the fans really rate him. His goal against Burnley was a beauty.

Of the **42** league goals that Newcastle United scored, **Rondon** and **Perez** scored or assisted **32** of them!

I smashed it on loan!

PLAYER OF THE YEAR

SALOMON RONDON

Rondon's header against AFC Bournemouth showed the fans what he's all about! He crashed a whipped cross home inside the box and went on to bag 11 league goals in the season, including two headers. It was a great deal when he joined on loan from West Bromwich Albion and his muscly displays up front made The Magpies tough to crack.

POSITION:	FORWARD
PREMIER LEAGUE GAMES:	32
PREMIER LEAGUE GOALS:	11
PASSES:	735
ASSISTS:	7
CROSSES:	14
RIGHT-FOOT GOALS:	5
LEFT-FOOT GOALS:	4
YELLOW CARDS:	1
RED CARDS:	0
FOULS:	22

The Cherries enjoyed another solid Premier League season in 2018–19. It's time to reveal the stars, style and secrets of Eddie Howe's south-coast side.

AFC BOURNEMOUTH

TEAM TALK

AFC Bournemouth started the season very well, losing just twice in their first ten league games. Callum Wilson and Josh King were one of the most impressive strike duos and Ryan Fraser and David Brooks were cool and creative in midfield. Injuries to Brooks, Wilson and captain Simon Francis hit The Cherries, but signings like Dominic Solanke and Chris Mepham stepped in to help the team.

SEASON STATS

POSITION: 14TH
PREMIER LEAGUE POINTS: 45
PREMIER LEAGUE WINS: 13
PREMIER LEAGUE GOALS SCORED: 56
PREMIER LEAGUE GOALS CONCEDED: 70
CLEAN SHEETS: 10
SHOTS: 446
PENALTIES SCORED: 7
PASSES: 15,943
CROSSES: 613
TACKLES: 526
YELLOW CARDS: 60
RED CARDS: 1
FOULS: 170
OFFSIDE: 57

MEGA MOMENT >>>>>>

AFC Bournemouth's 4–0 bashing of Chelsea was one of the best in their history! King's double, plus strikes from Brooks and Charlie Daniels, gave The Blues no chance and sent the home fans wild. The Cherries had less possession and made fewer passes, but getting the ball in the net is what really counted!

5 EPIC STARS

JOSH KING
Even though he went nine games without a goal, the Norway striker still had 12 goals to his name and scored doubles over Watford and Chelsea.

RYAN FRASER
Fraser forcing his way down the wings got the crowd on their feet at the Vitality Stadium! He was happy to shoot with either foot and racked up 14 assists.

DAVID BROOKS
He made the leap from Sheffield United in the Championship to the Premier League look easy. A creative midfielder with a talent for scoring and assisting.

JEFFERSON LERMA
Handled his £25 million price tag very well with a series of sick midfield displays. Lerma won 69 per cent of his tackles and made over 1,500 passes!

STEVE COOK
Clocking up his 300th Cherries appearance, the no-nonsense defender guided his side to eight clean sheets. He scored the winner at West Ham United, too.

Boom! Wicked Wilson strikes again!

Callum **Wilson** also scored on his England debut at Wembley against the USA in 2018.

PLAYER OF THE YEAR

CALLUM WILSON

By the end of the season, the England striker's overall Premier League record was a healthy 33 goals in 91 games. He reached that total with a mixture of right and left-foot strikes, headers and penalties. Wilson also made nine assists and averaged nearly 15 passes per game – he's an all-round team superstar for AFC Bournemouth!

POSITION:	FORWARD
PREMIER LEAGUE GAMES:	30
PREMIER LEAGUE GOALS:	14
PASSES:	440
ASSISTS:	9
CROSSES:	20
RIGHT-FOOT GOALS:	7
LEFT-FOOT GOALS:	3
YELLOW CARDS:	3
RED CARDS:	0
FOULS:	41

After a poor start, Burnley finally discovered their form to climb the table and keep away from danger. Discover the story of The Clarets' season.

BURNLEY

TEAM TALK

Manager Sean Dyche wasn't afraid to play with two strikers in a hardworking 4-4-2 formation, using Chris Wood and Ashley Barnes as his frontline. Joe Hart and Tom Heaton competed for the keeper's jersey and Johann Gudmundsson, Ashley Westwood and Jack Cork were charged with creating chances from midfield. James Tarkowski and Ben Mee were reliable at the back and youngster Dwight McNeil enjoyed a breakthrough year.

SEASON STATS

POSITION:	15TH
PREMIER LEAGUE POINTS:	40
PREMIER LEAGUE WINS:	11
PREMIER LEAGUE GOALS SCORED:	45
PREMIER LEAGUE GOALS CONCEDED:	68
CLEAN SHEETS:	8
SHOTS:	360
PENALTIES SCORED:	2
PASSES:	13,011
CROSSES:	693
TACKLES:	583
YELLOW CARDS:	75
RED CARDS:	1
FOULS:	172
OFFSIDE:	106

MEGA MOMENT > > > > >

A 1-0 win over Champions League-chasing Spurs in February sent the fans wild. The result also set a new Premier League record for Burnley, as they went eight games without defeat for the first time. On the back of three straight defeats around Christmas, this was a much-needed record for the Burnley boys!

5 EPIC STARS

CHRIS WOOD
Whether starting or making an impact from the bench, Wood put pressure on defenders with his strength and heading. He scored ten goals in 2018-19.

ASHLEY WESTWOOD
Westwood hit top gear in the second half of the season. He's a tough midfielder who loves chasing, tackling and setting up strikers. He made seven assists.

JAMES TARKOWSKI
Burnley's top centre-back made 71 tackles, 235 clearances and scored a huge winner against Brighton & Hove Albion at Turf Moor in December.

JOHANN GUDMUNDSSON
The ice-cool Iceland star was involved in nine Premier League goals and made 491 passes from midfield. An impact substitute, too.

DWIGHT McNEIL
The eye-catching winger enjoyed a great run in the team from December to help Burnley set a club record eight games unbeaten.

The Saints' eventful season finally saw them finish in 16th position and secure top-flight footy once again. See who starred for Southampton in 2018–19.

SOUTHAMPTON

TEAM TALK

Using three centre-backs and getting width from stars such as Valery and Bertrand, Southampton's well-drilled system and tactics really got the most out of their squad. Redmond sometimes supported main striker Ings, with Long and Austin useful additions from the bench. Alex McCarthy and Angus Gunn competed to become the club's first-choice keeper.

POSITION:	16TH
PREMIER LEAGUE POINTS:	39
PREMIER LEAGUE WINS:	12
PREMIER LEAGUE GOALS SCORED:	45
PREMIER LEAGUE GOALS CONCEDED:	65
CLEAN SHEETS:	7
SHOTS:	483
PENALTIES SCORED:	4
PASSES:	14,297
CROSSES:	664
TACKLES:	699
YELLOW CARDS:	71
RED CARDS:	3
FOULS:	217
OFFSIDE:	61

MEGA MOMENT > > > > > >

Although The Saints enjoyed their win over Arsenal, their 2–1 victory against another north London team was even better. On 9 March, Southampton grabbed three points from Spurs after coming back from behind for the first time in the season. Valery and Ward-Prowse both beat World Cup-winning keeper Hugo Lloris late in the second half.

PIERRE-EMILE HOJBJERG
Made captain by Ralph Hasenhuttl, the rock-hard midfielder is a fans' hero! The Dane collected seven yellow and two red cards.

JAN BEDNAREK
A key man in wins over Arsenal and Spurs, the defender linked up superbly with players such as Vestergaard, Yoshida and Stephens at the back.

NATHAN REDMOND
The exciting winger came to life in the second half of the season. He notched up six goals, four assists and made an average of almost 30 passes per match.

DANNY INGS
On loan from Liverpool FC, the striker had injuries but his goals helped to earn points against Crystal Palace, Brighton & Hove Albion, Arsenal and Huddersfield Town.

RYAN BERTRAND
Southampton were happy to see the left-back return to the team in February after injury. He gave the team a speedy attacking outlet down the wing.

COMING SOON:

NEW MATCH ATTAX APP!

TAKE ON YOUR FRIENDS!

Challenge your friends to a Match Attax match, whether you're hanging out together or miles apart! We'll keep track of your head-to-head record to reveal which friend is the ultimate Match Attax champion!

LIVE CARDS

These cards can only be found on the App. Attack and Defence stats will go up and down based on players' performances in real games!

FREE CODE IN EVERY PACK!

FREE TO DOWNLOAD!

Get it on your smartphone now!

WEEKLY TOURNAMENTS

Enter tournaments every week – take on players from all around the world and earn silverware to fill up your trophy cabinet!

HOW TO GET THE APP

You can now get the new Match Attax app to collect, swap and play with thousands of other fans! All you need to do is:

STEP 1: Search for "Match Attax" on your app store.

STEP 2: Download the new Match Attax App.

STEP 3: Scan codes found in Match Attax packets to get free digital cards.

STEP 4: Build your digital team and join the fun!

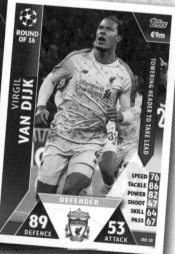

CELTIC'S GREAT EIGHT!

The Glasgow club stormed to their eighth league title in a row, holding off the challenge of city rivals Rangers. Here are the stats and stories from another super season in Scotland.

My goals were priceless!

CELTIC

Celtic wrapped up the championship in style, with manager Neil Lennon taking over from Brendan Rodgers in February. Striker Odsonne Edouard impressed, scoring 15 goals, and James Forrest, Scott Sinclair and Ryan Christie regularly hit the net. Keeper Scott Bain kept stacks of clean sheets in 2019 and Kieran Tierney, Kristoffer Ajer, Filip Benkovic, Mikael Lustig and ex-defender Dedryck Boyata helped to form a rock-hard defence.

SEASON STATS

CHAMPIONS: CELTIC
PREMIERSHIP TOP SCORER: ALFREDO MORELOS (RANGERS) 18 GOALS
PLAYER OF THE SEASON: JAMES FORREST (CELTIC)
BEST YOUNG PLAYER: ODSONNE EDOUARD (CELTIC)
SURPRISE TEAM: KILMARNOCK

RANGERS

Boss Steven Gerrard battled to get the better of Celtic in his first Premiership season. Morelos was his top scorer with 18 goals in the league and captain James Tavernier again did the business at right-back, chipping in with 14 strikes. Winger Ryan Kent caught the eye on loan from Liverpool FC.

Don't forget my 14 assists!

KILMARNOCK

Killie enjoyed a fabulous run at the start of the season and kept pace with the Glasgow clubs heading into Christmas. The highlight was their injury-time 2–1 win over the champions. Sadly their form dropped off and they slipped from the top two, but the likes of Greg Taylor, Eamonn Brophy, Gary Dicker and Alan Power can be very pleased with their season.

ABERDEEN

The Dons slipped two places from their 2018 finish, ending up behind Kilmarnock in fourth. Youngsters Lewis Ferguson, Sam Cosgrove and Scott McKenna were big stars for manager Derek McInnes. Cosgrove and Ferguson both netted in a dramatic 4–3 defeat at home to Celtic on Boxing Day!

PROMOTION PARTY!

Here's a reminder of who took the top spot and won promotion places in the Championship, League 1 and League 2!

CHAMPIONSHIP

Norwich City won the Championship in style! Teemu Pukki struck 29 to land the golden boot and Emiliano Buendia, Onel Hernandez and Marco Stiepermann became big stars. Norwich's never-say-die attitude summed up their team spirit and they came from behind to beat teams such as Nottingham Forest, Aston Villa, Rotherham United, Bristol City and Millwall. Sheffield United lost just twice in the league in 2019 to pip Yorkshire rivals Leeds United to automatic promotion, while Aston Villa went up thanks to a 2–1 victory over Derby County in the play-off final.

LEAGUE 1

The Hatters wrapped up the title on the last day of the season with a 3–1 win over Oxford United. Luton Town were the best team all season, losing only six games and finishing as top scorers with 90 goals. Barnsley bounced straight back to the Championship, earning an impressive 91 points and with losing just seven times. In the play-off final, Charlton Athletic's injury-time winner secured promotion, leaving Sunderland heartbroken.

Luton Town dropped out of the football league altogether between 2009 and 2014!

LEAGUE 2

Danny Cowley's well-drilled Lincoln City team were up as early as April 13 and pocketed the title nine days later. They had the second-best defence and attack in the division and stretched out a superb 19-game unbeaten run between late December and April to keep them at the top. Bury also know what it takes to clinch promotion to the third tier – it was the third time The Shakers had done it in the last nine seasons. MK Dons and Tranmere Rovers also went up.

These Premier League heroes need your help – some letters have been washed off their shirts! Under each player, write down what the name on each shirt should read.

MISSING LETTERS

I'm a champion at quizzes!

① RIC 41

ANSWER:..

② CHIL...L 3

ANSWER:..

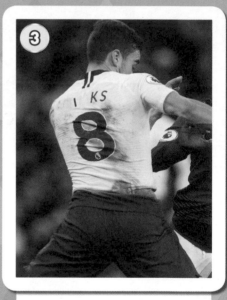

③ ...I KS 8

ANSWER:..

④ ALKE 2

ANSWER:..

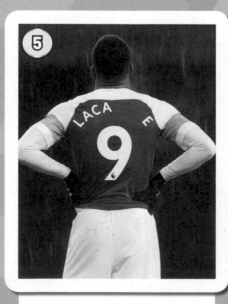

⑤ LACA...E 9

ANSWER:..

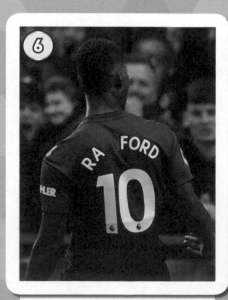

⑥ RA...FORD 10

ANSWER:..

7

ANSWER:...

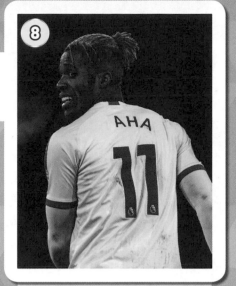

8

ANSWER:...

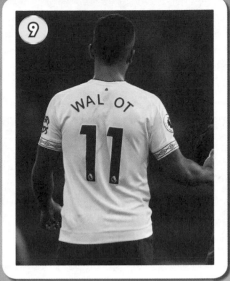

9

ANSWER:...

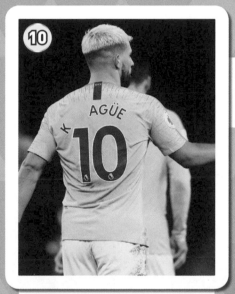

10

ANSWER:...

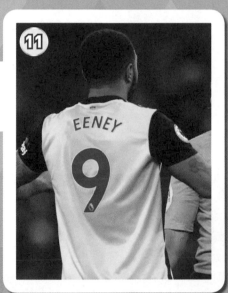

11

ANSWER:...

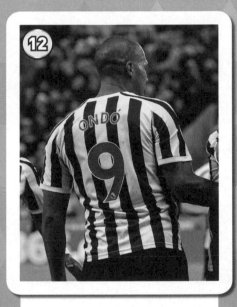

12

ANSWER:...

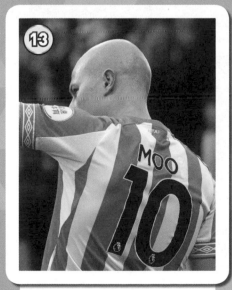

13

ANSWER:...

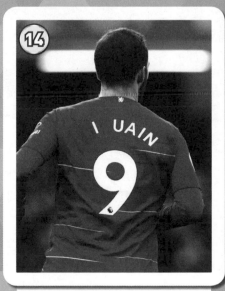

14

ANSWER:...

15

ANSWER:...

ANSWERS ON PAGE 55.

The Seagulls enjoyed their second Premier League season and battled hard to just beat the drop. Take a trip to the south coast to discover the story of their campaign.

BRIGHTON & HOVE ALBION

TEAM TALK

With players such as March, Knockaert and Izquierdo, Brighton & Hove Albion often attacked down the wings to get crosses over for Murray and Andone. Duffy and Dunk helped to keep their defence tighter than the likes of Burnley, Southampton, Cardiff City and Fulham in the table around them. Three 1-0 wins in a row in October gave the team a massive boost.

SEASON STATS

POSITION:	17TH
PREMIER LEAGUE POINTS:	36
PREMIER LEAGUE WINS:	9
PREMIER LEAGUE GOALS SCORED:	35
PREMIER LEAGUE GOALS CONCEDED:	60
CLEAN SHEETS:	7
SHOTS:	371
PENALTIES SCORED:	5
PASSES:	14,109
CROSSES:	636
TACKLES:	681
YELLOW CARDS:	60
RED CARDS:	4
FOULS:	235
OFFSIDE:	90

MEGA MOMENT > > > > >

The win over Manchester United was epic, but the fans loved beating rivals Crystal Palace 3-1 in December even more! In a crazy game at the Amex Stadium, The Seagulls played with ten men for 62 minutes but were 3-0 ahead at the break. Leon Balogun and Florin Andone bagged beauties as Brighton & Hove Albion made it six wins from 15 matches.

5 EPIC STARS

SHANE DUFFY
Tackles, blocks, headers, interceptions – Duffy bossed the backline and also bagged five goals as Brighton & Hove Albion beat the drop!

ANTHONY KNOCKAERT
The Frenchman was the team's creative star, scoring twice, setting up six goals in 2018–19 and making 107 crosses. Slick!

LEWIS DUNK
The no-nonsense centre-back played in all but two games for the club. Dunk made 42 tackles, 118 headed clearances and hit the net against Everton and Cardiff.

FLORIN ANDONE
Playing in a 'super sub' role, the striker scored a vital headed winner against Huddersfield Town after coming off the bench. A handful for defenders.

SOLLY MARCH
The hardworking left-winger marched on in 2018–19, making five assists and scoring once for The Seagulls. He missed just three games over the whole season.

Cardiff City fans loved their rollercoaster Premier League ride, even though it finished with the club sliding out of the division. Take a journey back over their season.

CARDIFF CITY

TEAM TALK

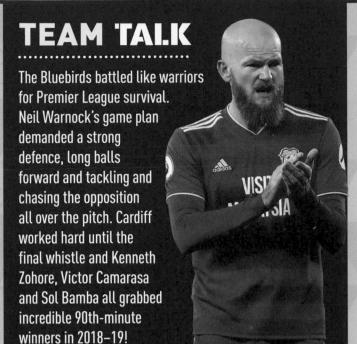

The Bluebirds battled like warriors for Premier League survival. Neil Warnock's game plan demanded a strong defence, long balls forward and tackling and chasing the opposition all over the pitch. Cardiff worked hard until the final whistle and Kenneth Zohore, Victor Camarasa and Sol Bamba all grabbed incredible 90th-minute winners in 2018–19!

SEASON STATS

POSITION:	18TH
PREMIER LEAGUE POINTS:	34
PREMIER LEAGUE WINS:	10
PREMIER LEAGUE GOALS SCORED:	34
PREMIER LEAGUE GOALS CONCEDED:	69
CLEAN SHEETS:	10
SHOTS:	417
PENALTIES SCORED:	3
PASSES:	10,226
CROSSES:	562
TACKLES:	655
YELLOW CARDS:	66
RED CARDS:	1
FOULS:	196
OFFSIDE:	77

MEGA MOMENT > > > > > >

Beating AFC Bournemouth 2–0 in February gave Cardiff City their first win of 2019, but it was also an emotional victory for the club. It was their first home game since new striker Emiliano Sala sadly died and fans at the Cardiff City Stadium paid their respects to the Argentine. Bobby Reid's double gave The Bluebirds all three points.

5 EPIC STARS

SOL BAMBA
With 175 clearances, 74 tackles, seven clean sheets and four goals, it was a huge blow when Bamba's season ended in March because of injury.

CALLUM PATERSON
Can play in defence or midfield, but in 2018–19 he mainly operated in attack and scored goals against Southampton, Brighton & Hove Albion and Fulham.

ARON GUNNARSSON
Cardiff's crunching midfielder is a defensive star. He protects The Bluebirds' back four and clocked up an impressive 749 passes last season in the Premier League.

HARRY ARTER
In defence or attack, Arter was an influential midfielder in 2018–19. He made 62 tackles and picked up ten yellow cards. He's a tough opponent!

VICTOR CAMARASA
On loan from La Liga club Real Betis, the Spaniard chipped in with five goals and four assists. A tidy and creative midfielder with a fabulous right foot.

Fulham were back in the Premier League after four years, but sadly didn't do enough to stay up. Here's the story of their campaign in west London.

FULHAM

I've got a Craven for goals!

TEAM TALK

After just one win in their first 12 league outings, Fulham knew they had to be much tougher at the back. They picked up wins over Southampton, Huddersfield Town and Brighton & Hove Albion with Aleksandar Mitrovic's goals doing the damage. Fulham spent over £50 million on key players Alfie Mawson and Andre-Frank Zambo Anguissa, but injuries hit their season.

POSITION: 19TH
PREMIER LEAGUE POINTS: 26
PREMIER LEAGUE WINS: 7
PREMIER LEAGUE GOALS SCORED: 34
PREMIER LEAGUE GOALS CONCEDED: 81
CLEAN SHEETS: 5
SHOTS: 454
PENALTIES SCORED: 2
PASSES: 17,699
CROSSES: 611
TACKLES: 591
YELLOW CARDS: 68
RED CARDS: 2
FOULS: 209
OFFSIDE: 90

MEGA MOMENT >> >> >

Fulham's exciting 3-2 win over Southampton was Claudio Ranieri's first game as manager before later being replaced by Scott Parker. It ended their run of six league losses in a row and gave the crowd hope they could escape the relegation zone. Their first clean sheet of the campaign, away at Newcastle United, was also one for the fans to cheer.

5 EPIC STARS

ANDRE SCHURRLE
The German World Cup winner brought class to Fulham's midfield. Schurrle got six goals, made 523 passes and 41 crosses into the box for the attackers.

CALUM CHAMBERS
Chambers enjoyed his new role as a defensive midfielder. In 2018-19 the ex-Arsenal man notched up 63 tackles and completed 1,484 passes.

RYAN SESSEGNON
The teenager's first Premier League season was full of exciting skills and hard work. The midfielder was involved in eight goals for Fulham in total.

JEAN MICHAEL SERI
The combative midfielder was a busy boy between the boxes. He won the official Premier League goal of the month in August for his strike against Burnley!

TOM CAIRNEY
The Cottagers' captain worked tirelessly in Fulham's effort to beat the drop. Cairney made 58 accurate long balls and won 129 duels in defence.

The Terriers lost their battle for Premier League survival in 2019. With their skilful squad they hope to make an instant return to the top flight!

HUDDERSFIELD TOWN

TEAM TALK

Huddersfield Town struggled for goals in 2018–19, scoring just 22 times. David Wagner was replaced with Jan Siewert in January as the club tried to turn things around. Laurent Depoitre, Aaron Mooy, Alex Pritchard, Steve Mounie and new signing Karlan Grant were their threats going forward as Christopher Schindler and Terence Kongolo stayed busy in defence. Captain Tommy Smith was troubled by injury.

SEASON STATS

POSITION: 20TH
PREMIER LEAGUE POINTS: 16
PREMIER LEAGUE WINS: 3
PREMIER LEAGUE GOALS SCORED: 22
PREMIER LEAGUE GOALS CONCEDED: 76
CLEAN SHEETS: 5
SHOTS: 400
PENALTIES SCORED: 1
PASSES: 15,902
CROSSES: 769
TACKLES: 710
YELLOW CARDS: 55
RED CARDS: 4
FOULS: 232
OFFSIDE: 63

MEGA MOMENT > > > > > >

Huddersfield Town's 2–0 win away to a quality Wolves side lifted them to 14th in the table. Mooy's double did the business and his second was a laser-guided free-kick past keeper Rui Patricio. The Terriers actually beat Wolves twice last season, picking up a fantastic 1–0 win in February after a last-gasp close-range strike by Mounie.

5 EPIC STARS

AARON MOOY
The creative Australian picked passes and threaded through balls. Mooy also had 43 shots and put 137 crosses into the box for The Terriers.

CHRISTOPHER SCHINDLER
The big German only missed one league game all season and his tackling, heading and interceptions were vital in central defence.

MATHIAS JORGENSEN
Known as Zanka, he was not only a key man at the back, but he also made an assist and scored against Leicester City, Brighton & Hove Albion and Manchester United.

STEVE MOUNIE
Mounie's main danger is his awesome aerial power. In 2018–19 he scored a sweet header against Burnley and also racked up three assists in the league.

JONATHAN HOGG
The popular defender won over 53 per cent of his tackles, made 72 defensive interceptions and won 31 aerial duels with the opposition.

SPOT THE DIFFERENCE

Circle the 10 differences between the two pictures.
Tick as you find them.

ANSWERS ON PAGE 55